RACIAL JUSTICE IN AMERICA
AAPI HISTORIES
ANGEL ISLAND IMMIGRATION STATION

T0061977

VIRGINIA LOH-HAGAN

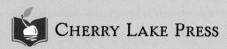
CHERRY LAKE PRESS

Published in the United States of America by Cherry Lake Publishing Group
Ann Arbor, Michigan
www.cherrylakepublishing.com

Reading Adviser: Beth Walker Gambro, MS, Ed., Reading Consultant, Yorkville, IL
Book Design and Cover Art: Felicia Macheske

Photo Credits: U.S. National Archives, Department of the Treasury. Public Health Service, Identifier: 176251230, 5; Library of Congress, Photo by J.D. Given, LOC Control No: 2007660596, 8-9; © Everett Collection Historical/Alamy Stock Photo, 7; © Allen.G/Shutterstock, 9; Official Map of Chinatown, PJ Mode Collection of Persuasive Cartography, 10-11; Library of Congress, Photo by Alfred A Hart, LOC Control No: 2005682948, 13; Library of Congress, Photo by Arnold Genthe, LOC Control No: 2018705060, 14; Library of Congress, Photo by Carol Highsmith, LOC Control No: 2013634670, 17; Library of Congress, Photo by Carol Highsmith, LOC Control No: 2013634664, 19; U.S. National Archives, Department of the Treasury. Public Health Service, Identifier: 176251228, 20; U.S. National Archives, Department of Commerce and Labor. Bureau of Immigration and Naturalization, Identifier: 176251228, 21; © Orangedrink/Shutterstock,23; © pixelheadphoto digitalskillet/Shutterstock, 25; Meiguoren/Wikimedia/Public Domain: commons.wikimedia.org/wiki/user:Meiguoren, 27; © Bumble Dee/Shutterstock, 29

Graphics Throughout: © debra hughes/Shutterstock

Cherry Lake Press is an imprint of Cherry Lake Publishing Group.

Library of Congress Cataloging-in-Publication Data

Names: Loh-Hagan, Virginia, author.
Title: Angel Island Immigration Station / by Virginia Loh-Hagan.
Description: Ann Arbor, Michigan : Cherry Lake Publishing, 2022.
  | Series: Racial justice in America: AAPI histories | Audience: Grades 4-6
Identifiers: LCCN 2022005352 | ISBN 9781668909294 (hardcover)
  | ISBN 9781668910894 (paperback) | ISBN 9781668912485 (ebook)
  | ISBN 9781668914076 (pdf)
Subjects: LCSH: Angel Island Immigration Station
  (Calif.)—History—Juvenile literature. | Angel Island
  (Calif.)—History—Juvenile literature. | United States—Emigration
  and immigration—Juvenile literature. | Race discrimination—United
  States—History—Juvenile literature. | United States—Ethnic
  relations—History—Juvenile literature.
Classification: LCC JV6926.A65 L63 2022 | DDC 304.8/73—dc23/eng/20220304
LC record available at https://lccn.loc.gov/2022005352

Cherry Lake Publishing Group would like to acknowledge the work of the Partnership for 21st Century Learning, a Network of Battelle for Kids. Please visit *http://www.battelleforkids.org/networks/p21* for more information.

Printed in the United States of America

Dr. Virginia Loh-Hagan is an author, former K-8 teacher, curriculum designer, and university professor. She's currently the director of the Asian Pacific Islander Desi American (APIDA) Center at San Diego State University. She is also the Co-Executive Director of the Asian American Education Project. She identifies as Chinese American and is committed to amplifying APIDA communities.

CHAPTER 1

What Was the Angel Island Immigration Station?

The Angel Island Immigration Station operated from 1910 to 1940. It's on the northern tip of Angel Island, which is located in the middle of the San Francisco Bay in California. It was the main port of entry for immigrants on the West Coast. It processed about half a million immigrants. The immigrants mostly came from Asian countries, including China, Japan, the Pacific Islands, Korea, and Vietnam. Non-Asian immigrants came from Australia, Russia, Canada, and South America.

Not all immigrants were treated the same. Upon arrival, immigrants were sorted and separated by their countries of birth. White and wealthy passengers were treated the best. They were processed aboard the ship and could go straight into San Francisco. They were welcomed into their new country.

Angel Island was called the "Ellis Island of the West." But the two immigration stations were very different.

Other immigrants were not welcomed so warmly. These included Asian immigrants and some Russian and Mexican people. They weren't allowed into San Francisco. They had to take a ferry to Angel Island. They were detained there and had to undergo more processing.

Anti-Chinese feelings were strong at this time. Chinese immigrants were treated the most unfairly. They were detained for longer periods at Angel Island. They had to overcome more barriers. They were treated like prisoners, but their only crime was being Chinese.

Think About It! Angel Island is farther away from the California coast than Alcatraz Island. Alcatraz was the location of a famous high-security prison. It was called "The Rock." No prisoner there had ever successfully escaped. How do you think being kept farther away than convicted prisoners made immigrants at Angel Island feel?

Some Russian immigrants experienced discrimination as part of the "Red Scare." Some Americans saw communist governments as a threat.

DID YOU KNOW...?

During World War II (1939-1945), Angel Island detained about 700 Japanese Americans. Their only crime was being of Japanese descent. They were detained for a few weeks. They were then sent to relocation camps on the West Coast. In 1941, Japan bombed Pearl Harbor Naval Base in Hawai'i. This action created anti-Japanese feelings. Many Japanese Americans were forced from their homes. The U.S. government said the reason for this action was national security. However, none of the detainees were found to be disloyal.

CHAPTER 2

What Is the History of Angel Island Immigration Station?

Before Angel Island, immigrants were processed and held in a shed in San Francisco. The shed was located at the Pacific Mail Steamship Company wharf. It was small, cramped, dirty, and unsafe.

The U.S. government needed a new immigration station. Officials wanted to inspect and detain Asian immigrants. They looked at Angel Island. Chinese community leaders were opposed. They didn't like how far away it was from San Francisco.

The Angel Island Immigration Station was called the "Guardian of the Western Gate."

IMMIGRATION STATION,
ANGEL ISLAND CAL.
COPYRIGHT 1915
J.D.Givens
1

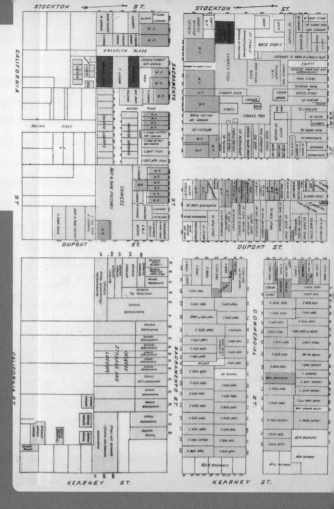

The construction of Angel Island Immigration Station began in 1905, but it was not used until 1910. It was expensive and not easy to manage. Everything had to be brought in by boat. The wooden buildings were fire hazards. In 1940, a fire destroyed the main office building. The 200 immigrants there at the time were moved to San Francisco.

In the 1960s, the Chinese American community fought to save the immigration station. They wanted to honor a history of hardships. They wanted to ensure a future that never forgets. Today, the Angel Island Immigration Station is a museum. Angel Island is a state park.

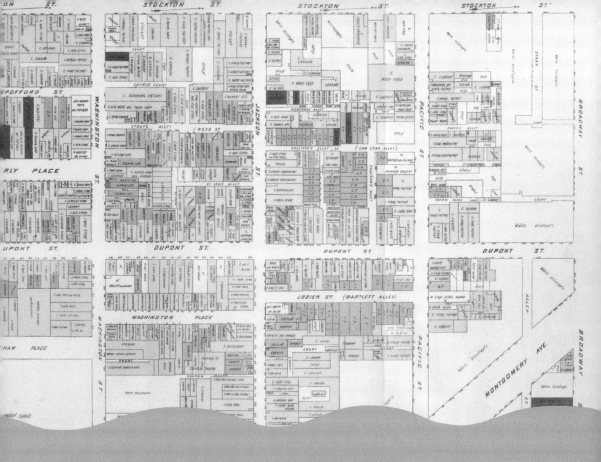

DID YOU KNOW...?

Chinese immigrants in San Francisco were forced to live in Chinatown. They were **excluded** from other parts of the city. Chinatown was poor and cramped. In 1900, there was a **bubonic plague** breakout. Officials **quarantined** Chinatown. Chinese immigrants weren't allowed to leave. But White Americans could come and go. At the time, Whites believed they were immune to the plague and that Chinese were spreading it. However, there was no proof of this belief. Chinese leaders hired lawyers. The court ruled in their favor and said restrictions had to apply to all.

CHAPTER 3

What Led to the Creation of the Angel Island Immigration Station?

The Angel Island Immigration Station's main purpose was to limit Chinese immigration. It was created to exclude Chinese immigrants because many Americans hated and feared them.

That wasn't always the case, though. At first, Chinese workers were welcomed. They were even recruited to come to the United States. In 1848, gold was discovered in California. Mining towns popped up. By the early 1860s, work had begun on the transcontinental railroad. This railroad connected the west and east coasts. Cheap labor was needed to build and maintain both the towns and the railroad.

People in southern China answered the call. In China, they faced floods and famine. The immigrants wanted better lives. They came to the United States hoping for freedom and fortune. Instead, they faced many hardships. Many died from explosions, landslides, and disease while building the railroads.

Despite the hardships they faced, Chinese workers were blamed for White workers losing their jobs. Newspapers labeled Chinese immigrants as dirty and dangerous. Chinese workers were seen as "perpetual foreigners" and outsiders. Their language, clothes, and traditions were seen as too foreign to fit in.

Think About It! In 1898, the Supreme Court ruled in favor of Wong Kim Ark. Ark was born in the United States to parents who were not citizens. This ruling granted U.S. citizenship to children born in the United States. Many schools don't teach about Wong Kim Ark or other important Asian Americans. Why do you think that is?

Chinese immigrants who worked on the transcontinental railroad were not given any credit for their contributions.

California passed several anti-Asian laws. Asian immigrants couldn't own land. Also, they couldn't marry someone of another race.

DID YOU KNOW...?

Denis Kearney was a California labor leader. He said, "The Chinese must go!" This became a popular slogan for "Yellow Peril." It was used in speeches, newspapers, and posters. It was used in rallies against Asian immigrants. Yellow Peril was an anti-Asian movement. It claimed that Asians were a threat to White purity. White people feared that Asians were taking over. The main purpose of Yellow Peril was to maintain White supremacy.

Politicians created laws excluding the immigrants. The Chinese Exclusion Act of 1882 had the most impact. This law banned Chinese workers from immigrating to the United States. This was the first time the United States excluded a specific cultural group.

In 1906, an earthquake and fires destroyed San Francisco. The main government building, city hall, burned to the ground. Immigration records were destroyed. Chinese immigrants used this as an opportunity to find loopholes in the unfair law. The Exclusion Act banned Chinese workers, but it allowed merchants to come and even bring their families.

Some Chinese in the United States claimed to be related to merchants or citizens. They claimed to have family in China. They created fake identities. They sold these identities to people in China. They were families on paper only. This created the "paper son" system.

People in China paid a lot of money for a paper son identity. They bypassed the Exclusion Act and immigrated. The United States tried to stop this system of fake identities by creating the Angel Island Immigration Station.

CHAPTER 4

What Happened At the Angel Island Immigration Station?

Chinese immigrants faced many difficulties at Angel Island. All Chinese immigrants were accused of being paper sons. They received very harsh treatment.

All immigrants had to pass medical exams. This was a very shameful experience for Chinese immigrants. They were tested, poked, and probed by doctors. Any sick immigrants were deported.

If immigrants passed the medical exams, they were assigned a bed. The living conditions were poor. The rooms were cramped and dirty. The immigrants were locked inside. Tall fences with barbed wire surrounded them. Guards were stationed everywhere. They inspected all belongings, including personal letters and packages.

Chinese immigrants ate in segregated dining halls. The tables were usually dirty. The food was not good. Sometimes immigrants rioted. They broke dishes and refused to eat.

The beds at Angel Island were stacked on top of each other.

The worst part were the interrogations. Chinese immigrants were detained for long periods. Some were there for 2 weeks. Some were there for 2 years.

Each immigrant had a hearing. The hearings were led by two interrogators. A stenographer and translator were also there. These officials spent many hours asking questions. Officials wanted to expose paper sons. The immigrants had to prove they were related to merchants or citizens. The officials asked questions about specific details over and over again. They compared the answers to those given by the U.S. family members. If answers were different, the immigrants were deported.

 Think About It! "Loneliness" is one of the words inscribed on the steps of the immigration center museum. Why is this an appropriate word to describe what happened at Angel Island? What other words come to your mind?

DID YOU KNOW...?

Chinese immigrants wrote poems and messages on the walls in Angel Island. Over the years, the walls were painted over. In 1931 to 1932, Smiley Jann and Tet Yee were detained at Angel Island. They copied the poems and saved these memories. These wall carvings are an important part of history. They tell the stories of many Chinese immigrants. After the fire in 1940, the station was scheduled to be destroyed. In 1970, Park Ranger Alexander Weiss toured the building. He saw the wall carvings. He helped pass a law to preserve Angel Island. Angel Island is now a national historical landmark.

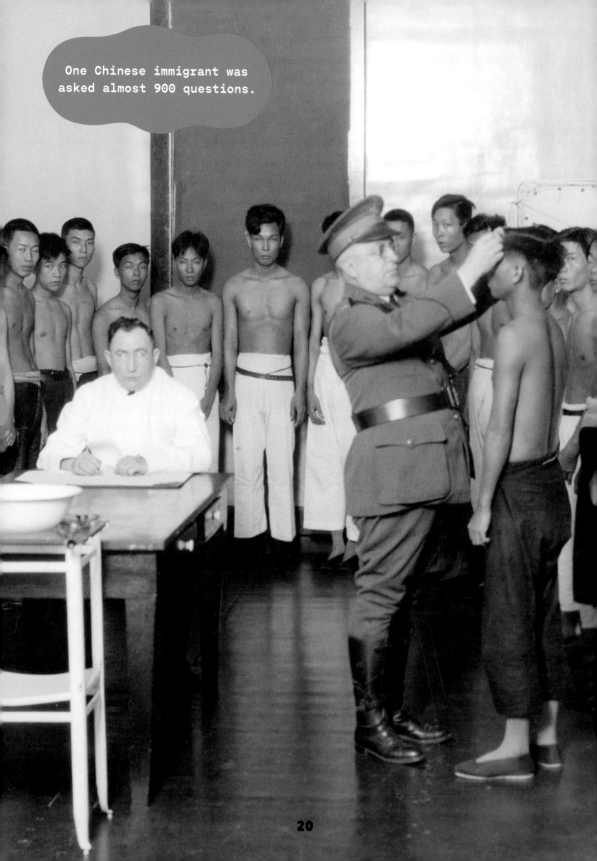

Coaching books were given to the paper sons. They contained details about their fake families. Everyone had to memorize these details. Before reaching San Francisco, paper sons threw their books into the ocean.

Officials tried to prevent cheating. Immigrants were isolated from the mainland. They weren't allowed visitors. Even the Angel Island staff was not allowed to talk to the people there. In some cases, paper families paid staff to pass on messages.

Think About It! The interrogators asked intense questions. They asked questions such as: "What are all the furniture pieces in your house? What are the birthdates of all your family members, including grandparents and cousins? What materials is your house made of?" Can you answer these questions? Would everyone in your family answer the same way?

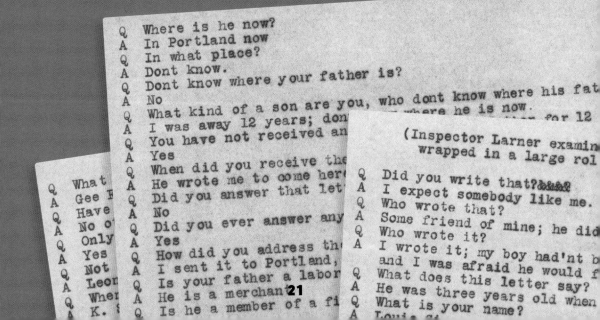

Q Where is he now?
A In Portland now
Q In what place?
A Dont know.
Q Dont know where your father is?
A No
Q What kind of a son are you, who dont know where his fat
A I was away 12 years; don   ere he is now.
Q You have not received an   for 12
A Yes
Q When did you receive the
A He wrote me to come here   Q Did you write that?
Q Did you answer that let   A I expect somebody like me.
A No   Q Who wrote that?
Q Did you ever answer any   A Some friend of mine; he did
A Yes   Q Who wrote it?
Q How did you address th   A I wrote it; my boy had'nt b
A I sent it to Portland,   and I was afraid he would f
Q Is your father a labor   Q What does this letter say?
A He is a merchan**21**   A He was three years old when
Q Is he a member of a fi   Q What is your name?

Q What
A Gee
Q Have
A No o
Q Only
A Yes
Q Not
A Leon
Q Wher
A K.

(Inspector Larner examin
        wrapped in a large rol

CHAPTER 5

What Happened after the Interrogations?

Chinese immigrants have suffered through a history of exclusion. The interrogations made Chinese immigrants suspicious. They mistrusted the government. They worried about being deported.

The United States tried a new way to end the paper son system. They created the Chinese **Confession** Program. This program took place from 1956 to 1965. The United States offered citizenship to paper sons, but paper sons had to confess their fake status.

Those who confessed had to give up their **passports**. They risked being deported. They had to share the names of everyone who helped them. They also had to share the names of their blood and paper families. This meant they risked deporting others as well. Only about

13,000 people confessed. Many more kept quiet. Paper sons didn't believe they'd be protected.

Think About It! Immigration laws are based on our relations with other countries. We do this to maintain peace and also to profit. In what other ways are we connected to other countries? Why is it important to develop relations with other countries?

Neighbors could also report people. This created fear and distrust in many Chinese communites.

The Chinese Exclusion Act led to other discriminatory laws. The 1917 Immigration Act created "Asian Barred Zones." This banned immigrants from Asian countries.

In the 1940s, the United States had a new enemy. The country fought against Japan in World War II. The U.S. government wanted China's support. This led to the 1943 Magnuson Act. This act repealed the Chinese Exclusion Act. It allowed some Chinese in the United States to become naturalized citizens.

President Franklin D. Roosevelt praised the Magnuson Act. He said it helped correct the "historic mistake" of Chinese exclusion. Many thought the act was a good thing. But it still had its flaws. Only 105 Chinese people could immigrate each year.

Asian exclusion ended with the 1952 Immigration Act. That act still had limits. It limited immigration by race instead of nation. The 1965 Immigration Act allowed in more skilled workers and family members. It got rid of bans based on race and nationality. It no longer gave preference to Europeans. The Chinese American community doubled in size because of this act. Also, more Asian Americans ran for office at this time. They fought to change laws.

The Magnuson Act increased immigration from the Philippines and India.

DID YOU KNOW...?

During World War II, many U.S. soldiers served overseas. They married women and had families overseas. But the immigration laws didn't let them bring their new families to the United States. Congress passed the 1945 War Brides Act to let in foreign wives and children of soldiers. At first, the act only served White and Black soldiers. Chinese American soldiers and their families won the right to immigrate later.

CHAPTER 6

What Is Still Happening Today?

The Chinese Exclusion Act was very harmful to the Chinese American community. It has affected generations of Chinese Americans. Experts say about one in three Chinese Americans today are connected to a paper son.

The paper son system impacted the paper sons' children and grandchildren. Paper sons didn't want to reveal themselves. They feared being deported. Many felt shame. They took on fake identities. This meant they had fake birthdays, fake family members, and fake names.

Family names are very important to the Chinese. Chinese people identify themselves as a member of their family first. They belong to the generations before and after them. Changing their names meant denying their ancestors. It meant changing their family histories. The descendants of paper sons carry the names of their paper families. Those born in the United States are citizens. Many are just learning about their paper son history. This has caused family tensions.

Paper sons weren't the only illegal immigrants. Thousands of other Chinese immigrants, mainly women, sneaked across the Canadian and Mexican borders.

中華會館

ASOCIACION CHINA DE MEXICALI ZONA CENTRO AV. JUAREZ 120

The Chinese Exclusion Act set a model for mistreating Asians. Because of it, Asian Americans felt like the "other." They became victims of hate crimes. The 1871 Chinese Massacre was an example. It took place in Los Angeles, California. A mob of 500 White Americans raided Chinatown. They hung 19 Chinese immigrants.

Anti-Asian hate still impacts Asian Americans. In 2019, the COVID-19 pandemic broke out. It was called the "Kung Flu" and the "China Virus." Such comments spread hate. Hate crimes against Asian Americans increased by 150 percent. In 2021, there was a shooting in Atlanta, Georgia. Six Asian American women were killed.

The Chinese Exclusion Act continues to impact immigration conversations. It raised questions about who should be allowed to immigrate. Immigration is still a big issue today. Undocumented immigrants are those living in the United States without proper papers. Their plight is similar to paper sons. The United States continues to grapple with immigration issues.

Most of the undocumented Asian immigrants live in California and New York. Most come from India and China.

DID YOU KNOW...?

Tyrus Wong lived from 1910 to 2016. He's famous for being an artist. He worked on Disney movies like *Bambi*. He was also a paper son. His birth name was Wong Gen Yeo. His paper son name was Look Tai Yow. His White teachers changed his name to Tyrus. At age 9, he left China on the S.S. *China*. He sailed to the United States with his family. He was detained and interrogated at Angel Island. After a month, he and his father were released. They moved first to Sacramento, California, and then to Los Angeles. Wong never saw his mother and sister again.

SHOW WHAT YOU KNOW!

A major injustice happened at the Angel Island Immigration Station. People of Chinese descent were detained unfairly. Let's work to never let this happen again.

Research Ellis Island. Ellis Island was an immigration station from 1892 to 1954. It processed more than 12 million immigrants. Most of the immigrants were from Europe. These immigrants had a different experience from the Chinese immigrants at Angel Island. Ellis Island was known as a welcoming place. Angel Island was not. Compare and contrast Angel Island and Ellis Island. Focus on how they were different.

Show what you know! Choose one or more of these activities:

- Review firsthand accounts from Ellis Island and Angel Island. Pretend two immigrants from both places are having dinner together. Write a script of what they would say to each other. Film it.

- Pretend you're a newspaper reporter from the early 1900s. Write an article about Angel Island.

- Read all the books in the *Racial Justice in America* series. Create a journal, podcast, or social media campaign. Include a segment about Angel Island.

Think About It! Think about all the things you have learned. What would you like to learn more about?

SHOW WHAT YOU CAN DO!

Share your learning. Being an ally is the first step in racial justice work. Allies recognize their privilege. We all come from different positions of privilege. We also have different types of privilege. In the United States, being White is a privilege. Other examples include being male or an English speaker.

Use your privileges to help all achieve equality. Angel Island taught us that we have unfair laws and practices. It showed us that we need to treat immigrants better. Here are ways you can be an ally:

- Treat immigrants with respect. Thank them for the work they do. Make them feel welcome.

- Fight to make sure all immigrants have the same rights as you. Support laws that promote immigrants' rights.

- Volunteer to help refugees. Teach English. Provide childcare. Listen to their stories.

We all have a role to play in racial injustice. We also have a role in making a better world. Do your part. Commit to racial justice!

Think About It! Think about your privileges. Do you want to improve the lives of others? What are you willing to give up to do this?

EXTEND YOUR LEARNING

FICTION

James, Helen Foster, and Virginia Shin-Mui Loh. *Paper Son: Lee's Journey to America*. Ann Arbor, MI: Sleeping Bear Press, 2013.

NONFICTION

Loh-Hagan, Virginia. *A is for Asian American: An Asian Pacific Islander Desi American Alphabet Book*. Ann Arbor, MI: Sleeping Bear Press, 2022.

Loh-Hagan, Virginia. *Detained and Interrogated: Angel Island Immigration*. Ann Arbor, MI: Cherry Lake Publishing, 2020.

Public Broadcasting Service: Asian Americans
https://www.pbs.org/weta/asian-americans

GLOSSARY

ally (AH-lye) a person who is aware of their privilege and supports oppressed communities

ancestors (AN-seh-stuhrz) family members who lived in an earlier time

bubonic plague (byoo-BAH-nik PLAYG) a deadly disease

communist (KAHM-yuh-nist) a type of government where all property is owned by the government and profits are shared by all

confession (kuhn-FEH-shuhn) the act of admitting or telling one's sins

deported (dih-POR-tuhd) sent a person back to their country of birth

descendants (dih-SEHN-duhnts) members of the future generation of people

detained (dih-TAYND) jailed or held in police custody

excluded (ik-SKLOOD-uhd) kept out or denied access to

famine (FAH-muhn) extreme, widespread shortage of food

ferry (FEHR-ee) a small boat used for short trips to and from a place

hearing (HEER-ing) a trial that allows a person to state one's case

interrogations (in-ter-uh-GAY-shuhnz) long, official questioning sessions

loopholes (LOOP-holz) mistakes in the way a law or rule is written that makes it possible to avoid obeying it

massacre (MAH-sih-kuhr) the killing of a large number of people in a cruel and violent manner

naturalized (NAH-chuh-ruh-lyzd) citizenship granted to a person who was born in a different country

pandemic (pan-DEH-mik) an epidemic spread over multiple countries or continents

passports (PASS-ports) official documents showing that the holder is a citizen of a country and has the right to travel to other countries

peril (PEHR-uhl) danger

perpetual (puhr-PEH-chuh-wuhl) never-ending

privilege (PRIV-lij) a special, unearned right or advantage given to a chosen person or group

quarantined (KWOR-uhn-teend) held in isolation to prevent the spread of disease

refugees (reh-fyoo-JEES) people forced to leave their countries to escape war, natural disasters, or other dangers

repealed (rih-PEELD) to have been officially cancelled

segregated (SEH-grih-gay-tuhd) separated, usually by race or gender

stenographer (stuh-NAH-gruh-fuhr) a person who takes notes

translator (TRANS-lay-tuhr) a person who interprets what someone says from one language to another

undocumented (uhn-DAH-kyuh-men-tuhd) referring to people living in a country without legal papers

virus (VYE-ruhs) a type of germ that can make people sick

INDEX